ALSO BY LEE SEONG-BOK

Indeterminate Inflorescence

Ah, Mouthless Things

I Heard Life Calling Me

THAT SUMMER'S END

THAT SUMMER'S END

POEMS

Lee Seong-bok

TRANSLATED BY ANTON HUR

ALFRED A. KNOPF NEW YORK 2026

A BORZOI BOOK
FIRST HARDCOVER EDITION
PUBLISHED BY ALFRED A. KNOPF 2026

Published by Alfred A. Knopf, a division of Penguin Random House LLC,
1745 Broadway, New York, NY 10019.
Originally published in South Korea by Moonji Publishing Co., Ltd. in 1990.

"Encounter," "Taboo," "Before Getting Dark 1," "Before Getting Dark 2," and "Street" originally appeared in the *New England Review.*
This translation was funded in part by a grant from the Daesan Foundation.

Library of Congress Cataloging-in-Publication Data
Names: Yi, Sŏng-bok, [date], Author. | Hur, Anton, Translator.
Title: That summer's end : poems / Lee Seong-bok ; translated by Anton Hur.
Other titles: Kŭ yŏrŭm ŭi kkŭt. English.
Description: First hardcover edition. | New York : Alfred A. Knopf, 2026.
Identifiers: LCCN 2025038296 |
ISBN 9780593804032 (hardcover) | ISBN 9780593804049 (ebook)
Subjects: LCGFT: Poetry.
Classification: LCC PL992.9.S6268 K813 2026
LC record available at https://lccn.loc.gov/2025038296

penguinrandomhouse.com | aaknopf.com

Printed in Canada
1st Printing

The authorized representative in the EU for product safety and compliance is Penguin Random House Ireland, Morrison Chambers, 32 Nassau Street, Dublin D02 YH68, Ireland, https://eu-contact.penguin.ie.

TO MY DAUGHTER,

Suyu

CONTENTS

THAT SUMMER'S END

FEELING

How do feelings come
a bough first blossoms
Is that how feelings come
a bough first drops its blossoms
Is that how feelings fall

A droplet on a page
lingers long before
drying to a blot
a warp on paper
an indelible trace

ENCOUNTER

My mind is a valley   deep and shaded   birds and beasts in every fold   I have sought bright places only   when I sought the light no more my mind grew lighter   the birdsongs and beastcries stirred me from sleep   when did you slip inside

WESTERN SEA

I've never been to the western sea
You may be there for all I know

How different can it be from other seas
Tiny crabs crawling in and out of their holes
the sea off thrashing against the mudflats

For your sake
I keep it the one place I won't go
if I go everywhere there's nowhere you might be

A bit of sea I never go to
tumbling always in my mind

TABOO

Still I am not free
Within me are many taboos
Even the attainable I'm told is forbidden

Perhaps you are my taboo
Has giving me a taboo
given you freedom

Like a twisted zelkova branch
casting its shadow on my roof
you never part from me

FISH

From a very close place I saw you and lay where you had lain the sky was so blue enough for chills the occasional sound of your breath also blue

I think of the place you will lay me down for my rest the place where I wake thirsty in the early morning and the golden fish have vanished

The rising fish too pained and lost to hide the place where our golden fish had gone . . .

FLOWERING DAYS

Even from afar I know you
Deaf and blind you wander the cold underground
and try to be the small smile on someone's lips

Even without calling you come
without being thought or dreamed of
Even the dry mound of dirt rears its head

You are now inside of me
And not knowing of me
you struggle to slough me off

When you leave me
my throat will split and veins burst and
my eyes, my ears, my ragged body shred

I'll want to cry, want to laugh, want to vomit
gulp down a bowl of water and scream in hysterics
you paler softer than a flower tteok I'll spit out in petals

The thought of releasing you as I crumble darkens me
I dread kindling the stiffening skin
Rebirth piercing this burnt skin like a dream

Now you are inside me but I
don’t know how to release you
tiny hands ripping my heart, your stomping feet

TWO FLOWERING TREES

Two flowering trees were in your garden One had pretty leaves the other lush branches

Seeing me linger before them you invited me to take one

I wanted both To plant one in the yard and the other by the door

Even knowing your garden would be bare, that you'd sicken from emptiness . . .

Two flowering trees were in your garden you smiled in sorrow between them

BEFORE GETTING DARK 1

Pointing to the darkening mountain you said Look azaleas There and there Wherever you pointed in surprise bloomed flowers dipped in darkness and blood

If you called me then on that dark cliff I would've bloomed for the first time

BEFORE GETTING DARK 2

Dripping their watercolors the flowering trees
walk in a line
Their modest lantern parade unending

Where were we going
Our wedding clothes smeared with deathly light
Everyone laughing in fragrant white

Where were we
Before it got too dark
I saw you again and again

Before it got dark
my sight dimmed and
in the lines of flowering trees I saw you not

STREET

What I loved sometimes repulsed me so
it infuriated
Trees rumpled with blossoms by my head
that droop

What I loved sometimes repulsed me so
that I set out on the frozen streets
and there was a child with a ring rash
asleep on the back of a mother by her molasses

What I loved sometimes repulsed me so
that I tried to leave but
I'm asleep on Mother's back
as she stands by her molasses for sale

SEA

Sorrow called to me
I didn't answer

Sorrow followed me
I didn't flee
together we went on a long trek

Pine forests obscured my view
in them sorrow hid
after a moment's wait
I glimpsed it stepping forth

Its back a dark blue bend
and white froth in its mouth   sorrow, O
sorrow rushed toward me
Even as it fell and shattered, it waved

HOME

We build our brick-and-mortar homes but hesitate on the threshold because the home of the mind is far away Even if we find the home of the mind we hesitate on the threshold because what we call home left long ago in search of what it calls home

The more we empty our home the heavier it becomes and the closer we get to it the farther!

MOUNTAIN

This world holds the dirtiest gutters people ever lived in and the neatest trees no human hand touches   In this world both exist   But are not together and must be sought out   Between the two are hidden paths and time

THE MOUNTAIN NEARBY

I didn't know the mountain nearby was so deep Didn't know the mountain nearby where I took the children was so deep Not until I first went to the nearby mountain to see the winter trees The nearby mountain was not my neighborhood mountain The winding green of the mountains spills forth like an avalanche into the eastern and western seas I didn't know the mountain nearby was so deep Didn't know the mountain nearby where I took the children was so deep I wanted to ride the black wave of mountains to the eastern and western seas

MOUNTAIN PATH 1

The acacia trees had leaves so thick they tapped my forehead and shoulders and felt limitless Then the path stopped and I stood atop a cliff's edge

I've stood here before and know it well but every time I can't help the regret as I turn back

MOUNTAIN PATH 2

On a path barely wide enough for one   the acacia grew thick and the sunlight dappled   The path looked blocked   Thinking my way lost, I continued step by step into the pathless forest

Many times have I made it trembling back down that hard mountain path   Every time I thought the path was at an end it began again

MOUNTAIN PATH 3

It was a cliff cut into mountain but the only way past was to climb it When I placed a hand on the smooth cliff and pulled my body up the rock gave way Whenever my hand on the mountain trembled and slipped the deep fall below rushed toward me When I pushed my bloody hands between the rocks the mountain came into my grasp again and I climbed another step

MOUNTAIN PATH 4

The steep hill was full of rocks Among the layers of split rocks grew a young tree No matter how I chipped at the rock or dug with my hands it refused to reveal its roots As I grabbed its young trunk and pulled with all my might, the middle of the root snapped and bled a clear sap

At home I planted and watered it but the young tree still bled Our house by that bleeding young tree became more like that rough and rocky hill

MOUNTAIN PATH 5

The sunlight this morning was very hot We tried to stop you but you couldn't be stopped You hiked up the mountain path broken by last year's rains and turned to us and gestured That we should turn back . . . Whenever you fell you grabbed a tuft of grass and stood back up as stones the size of fists rolled and a red pillar of dust arose Several times you heaved yourself up and hid yourself from the heat inside the forest of twisted trees All that was left to see was a mountain path as tattered as an ox's back After you left the path became clearer Like a sob that ended long ago . . . it flowed down

IN THE FOREST

The forest was canopied with cicada cries
brimming with the throb of puny, winged torsos

When I approached their cries ceased
A few steps back and their shining song
between the leaves and shards of sun resumed

I could catch one if I tried
When caught the trapped forest will hold its breath
and my secret joy will be at an end

When I left the cicada cries shimmered
Their song at summer's dusk tore at my ears

FOREST 1

Above a windy forest lay another
forest bending sickly with the wind

The birds that turned as they dropped
clung on as if having seen the unspeakable

Above a windy forest lay another
forest drifting away once more

The forest grew lush with no other wounds
growing green like the grave mound of time

FOREST 2

After one ruckus
begins another
The silent forest vibrates

Suffering was always
new suffering

After one struggle
begins another
The forest is erased, suffering remains

Did suffering bury the forest
Did the forest leave suffering

Sometimes, when it wakes,
the forest smiles
pale

FOREST 3

In the morning a thin rain fell
and there were birds
returning with wet wings

The forest that clamored all that day
birthed nothing
The next day and the next, it
birthed nothing

When the wind finished sleeping,
the forest, perhaps shy
was still

TREE 1

The base of the maple tree was so pretty I kissed it repeatedly The slight salt of its bark stayed on my tongue

I wanted to live like that to shoulder the stream that pours into the valley to search between the rocks with my tender root

I wanted someday to snip out my own small sky to hang my skittish young leaves above what grew before

Did the maple tree bark know the slight salt of my kiss?

TREE 2

When I climb to a tall branch and swing off it, my swing becomes the tree's swing and it's hard to tell whether it's me or the tree swinging The young leaves danced with joy

Then I fell to the ground Thankfully, I wasn't hurt, but the torn branch hung so sadly, I tried to rip it off but its tough bark resisted

The bent tree leaned to the ground and the leaves danced unawares When I approached they turned their cheeks and writhed

TREE 3

It was tinged with green where life once resided The tree that had died this past winter I'd brought inside I stared at it for a long time Its roots were broken, its body parched, but still touched with green where life had passed

I heard its sobs that no one had before
The green hint of the dead tree's endless grief

RIVER 1

They say I look lonely
because on evenings when the dusk unfurls
I chase the poplar forest

They say I look sick
because my face has been blackened
by exhaust

Never was I lonely or sick
It was only that I'd rushed through
their cities

Never do I stop what comes
Never do I stop what goes
I am the tears that flow in their eyes

RIVER 2

The direction the river flowed
was unknowable
from watching only
the calm motion of the surface
Leaning on the shoulders of distant hills
did the river flow

But the sand left behind
ground fine by the great water passing
Where we ceased the river flowed still
past lives that were all but sand . . .

RIVER 3

Again came spring and grass thickened on the bank
The mountains sank and let down their hair
The tiny fish swimming between the detergent bubbles
opened their mouths   A hot thing
brushed past the indifferent leaves   Upon the edges
of my head and feet was a trickle of hate
The mountains sank and let down their hair
The city sent up sooty smoke
Again came spring and grass thickened on the bank

ON THE RIVERBANK

The morning rapids were unusually fast   In the shallows we washed our hair and faces

At lunch the bank where we'd played was empty   A fog of people had formed at the river bend where the water deepened

Was it death or the shadow of death, the drifting boat

Having found no body, the boat went on ferrying and newcomers began to play on the riverbank

CROSSING THE WATER 1

A child on the back of an older poet and another child on mine, we ventured where the water was deep With no strength in my legs and overcome by the rapids, my bulging eyes threatened to flee The older poet said to take smaller, ever smaller steps The water came up to my navel and above my nipples and whenever I slipped the child on my back barked a short shout After much stumbling came sudden calm, and when the water dropped below my navel I felt I had crossed over

CROSSING THE WATER 2

The wind blasts and the other shore is far but a few make progress   The water ought to be up to their necks by now but the women's fluttering skirts might mean it's only at their knees   A few steps up and over are three or four of them, linking arms to advance in the wind-frothed water   Now they are frozen in place and yelp when pushed, and the wind ripples the water and makes us blink, and the three or four women embracing resemble a palace of green reeds

CLIFF

Below are the rocks that dropped and smashed to become islands, and the waves that bite and rip without aid of teeth or tongue, and the froth that swirls and wanders where a frost-ridden seagull must have crashed against the rocks to become more foam, and from our omnipotent height where all can be lifted and felled we stand with a death that will gut us   Whether or not we fall and strike our bare heads against the crimson brink, the rock fragment islands sing their aching call for us and the afterlife calm of the water's deep color draws us in, and the trees that heave as they crawl up the hair-raisingly steep cliff face at dusk shiver with each shimmeringly blue inhale, exhale only to erase themselves within!

MEMORIES OF A VERY OVERCAST DAY

Birds flock by as they cover this place with graves

With the force of pushing a coffin lid I stare up at the sky

BURL

We have come here to realize how trivial we are to such trivial things as grass or insects Until we leave here we'll never realize it Like a hardened burl stuck on a piece of deadwood . . .

HAND

A hand, an other's hand, a hand older than their face approaches your chest   Never have you reached out to hold it, the gaunt hand of an other

CAT

A cat the size of a fist grooms its feet   It cares not for the gaze of others whether it grooms its toes or padded soles   A middle school student waiting for the bus offers their sneakered foot but the cat turns away, uninterested

I keep gazing at a life being lived   A very low life between the toes and the soles   A thing like a scratch that tickles as it begins to heal

TRAIN

The train stood still for thirty seconds or a minute before sliding away just as we let down our guard I turn to avoid showing it my desolate back and when the train is darkly far, memories like night snow, neither white nor dim, fall for three months and ten days, and as I linger where the train had left, for no other destination comes to mind, the train goes yet farther into the dark but does not disappear Perhaps the train has come to a stop No, it lingers only briefly for it pities us but will eventually disappear From suffering into the land of rivers, to the valley of forgotten tongues . . .

YOU

I drove out early in the morning and saw women dig the frozen ground to plant turnip seeds The children they carried on their backs lolled their heads in sleep The men were nowhere to be seen Fire simmered on the fields and swept the skies in white smoke

I followed the dirt path and met you Wearing boots that came up to your knees, you dug up lotus roots covered in earth from a mudflat

Was what you really found your wound, tougher and stiffer than any lotus root Was not what disappeared through the hollow water vessels of the lotus tubers, snapped in half by your shovel, a life of fruitless labor No matter how much I shouted you kept stabbing with your shovel and digging up frozen lotus roots

CHILD

My child goes up the high staircase
and looks down at me
Such height is the child's pride
but my anxiety

Our gazes meet over the years between us
and someday my sight will go
We shall never hold hands again

GIRLS

How could there be a stain on their laughter
Their laughter is inside the stain

Inside the sweaty midsummer bus
the girls laugh and laugh

Their laughter is like the ribs of a fan
whipped open for the first time

Whenever they laugh, a rib
snaps out, one by one

How could there be no years in laughter
The years lie dormant beneath their glee

MOTHER 1

The path to Mother is thick with growth and hard to trace   If I don't go now, Mother will worry and look for me as she hacks through the growth   but the path has scattered in the air and Mother and I wander lost all night through the thick forest

MOTHER 2

In the moonless night my mother slept in the tall grass and woke up with a fright but didn't want to wake me so she silently stamped her feet and I woke up in surprise to realize she was in the next room

Mother, how could one of us be in the grave and the other outside of it

ISLAND

An island met another island and had a child   Through the wide ocean the child island wandered, resenting the mother island and father island . . . The islands it met in its wanderings were each lonely   and when it first realized the gladness of loneliness the child island rushed quickly, quickly back   The mother island and father island had long since sunk in the sea

STAR

In the dark sky a single star trembles The birds fly low and the beasts move in herds to hide themselves The star is in danger, there is no place for it to hide The insects cry low and a flash of dry lightning drifts on the fast wind The star is panting, there's no place for it to run, soon it will be swallowed by crazy clouds! In the dark sky a single star trembles

WALL

A redbrick wall that allows not a vine to cling to it A whimper of anguish escapes The pained cry of not being able to knock down or burn this wall I want to hang on to this redbrick wall that allows not a vine to cling to it Before this dusty red wall of silence and shouting, I want to burn naked

COMMENTARY ON THE I CHING 1

For days I did not eat meat   The crying beasts made me sad, you see   Then one day, I ate meat   I made generous cuts of it to cook and it was delicious   They told me it came from the body of a spy executed that morning   I vomited for a long time and when I lifted my head   a world with a bloody mouth was chewing at some meat

COMMENTARY ON THE I CHING 2

Suddenly a caterpillar-like thing crawled on my left wrist so I hurriedly slapped it with my right hand but it didn't budge so I tried to pluck it off at least but I managed only to rip off its hairy hide and it burrowed deep into my wrist and would not separate from the flesh   Frightened, I rubbed my eyes and looked again, but it was gone, and I heard only the countless hairy critters silently, silently crawling inside my chest

COMMENTARY ON THE I CHING 3

Our child plays in his underwear outside but then is frightened and I see there is a boar much bigger than he is running toward him with its quiver-like snout up and I strike it down hard with a rod but it doesn't budge so I swing many times with an ax someone handed me and when I look down at the ax wounds on the shoulders and the bloody underwear in tatters I see what's really bloodied is our child

WILDFLOWER

Wildflower, my son says he feels sad when he hears your song My family, born with a wellspring of sadness, remembers you The bloody tattered flesh in the yellowed ID photos, the broken ribs captured in the X-rays, the silent gun barrel aimed down at the horse with the broken femur, the herded youth lined up against a wall waiting to be shot, no one saw any of this but . . . Wildflower, my son says he feels sad when he hears your song My family, born with a wellspring of sadness, remembers you

LOW SONG 1

My Lord, the bed that is my bride is drenched O water flowing close to the origin, my waiting trickled low to make two clear lakes But your two eyes, named mystery and mystery, the rinsed and rust-brown pebbles in the depths, I have also seen My Lord, but my waiting shall trickle low and dissipate All but for my Lord bride

LOW SONG 2

My Lord, who stands at the other end of this passage of joy, until now I was surely like a blocked cave   What bloomed forth from me, spring to summer, were traces of you   My Lord, I go to you now and pledge to become a cave that leaks to the light   At that other end of the passage, where joy flows like water, My Lord, this blocked capillary of yours, from spring to summer, now opens

LOW SONG 3

Hinge flowers or the like, a herd of antelope ran in search of these tiny blossoms   They couldn't eat them or chew them, and the petals were so small they were invisible, but if a blossom happened to shine in their eye, My Lord, is that when your endeavors came to an end   When the antelope cross the desert, against the sandstorms, on their burning feet, and their bones show through their hides, My Lord, are you a low song heard only by their ears

SILK ROAD 1

As a faraway ocean pushes into deep land
you came to me
As a strange dream that came with the deep night
you left me

One day the waves that accosted me calmed
and like the tranquil shadows of the trees
that grew below them
a longing that resembles you appeared
The winds blow and the waves accost
but it will not be erased

SILK ROAD 2

You were the water's shimmer at dusk that filled my eye
A thing like an endless tunnel deepened in me
When I turned, beads of clear water rolled down your forehead
I did not know it was a punishment at first
I did not know my suffering was your punishment
O, you were the water's shimmer at dusk that filled my eye

SILK ROAD 3

I saw a fortune-teller
who told me to claim you with haste
I did not know this would imprison you
You exhausted yourself to sleep against the tight weave of my pain
and I am like the butterfly net the neighborhood children threw away
Hurry, hurry and claim you, the people said
I did not know this would imprison you

SILK ROAD 4

When the jeotdae flute begins the blood beats and the body,
in some faraway place like India or Western Asia, sinks deep, deeper
There is only sand This flesh, these bones, this endless silk road . . .
As the jeotdae climaxed in its song, I saw you You, who are erased
when you turn in the slightest You, in your flesh made only of sand,
in endless tears

SILK ROAD 5

Like a puddle after rain you shall be
at the other side of my waiting   A worm in the mud, or rainwater
reflecting the sky after a storm . . .
All these insignificant things   I know now as your gaze

NEAR YOU 1

The reeds that suffer the wind
bump each other's shins
Some of them stand with crushed legs

Near you
the sunlight plays all day
and the crushed-shin things keep trying to stand
Over the mud of melted snow the roots squirm
And near you the sunlight plays all day

NEAR YOU 2

I keep raising my heels
but can't see you
Sometimes when wait lengthens
resentment rises
In the faraway sky cirrus clouds
float by What song could I sing
to reach your ear
We have never met and
therefore cannot part but even
unparted my hand is not in yours
and so the waiting deepens
and resentment rises

NEAR YOU 3

The trunk's bark keeps splitting and
illegible letters carve themselves in

We know of nothing aside
from our eating and dressing

We pick up the broken branch
and strike the unharmed tree

and all the scrawny branches
quiver and cower

Allow just one letter
Allow, to us, just one letter

Rubbing our muddy shoes on dry grass
we think of the walk back

NEAR YOU 4

I took the long way back
to where you are
and where the winter trees stood
I stood

If I learned your secret
would I become your secret too
A secret as soft as a snowflake
is that inside me too

Now like a cairn
by a forgotten stream
I am abandoned

speaking your name
in the light rain or
a brush of wind

NEAR YOU 5

The sunlight played all day near you
and at sunset wandered the hill behind the houses

Little did I know that to be led
by myths and premonitions and the like
was to be chased by them

O, the traces of legends,
I was chased by such things
and when tired, I too stood
where the winter trees were lined

receiving their leafless breath until
a shoulder was gouged by the wind

ON THE RIVERBANK 1

When I heard your voice and came out to the riverbank the sky stretched from the faraway hill green with spring grasses to the sandy crescent where I stood   The river was a single jaunty strand   The waves refused, gently, to depart   The mumble of the sand dragging in and pushing out, your embrace was too deep for me to flow in   The river curved behind the hill and out of sight, just as the last I saw of you

ON THE RIVERBANK 2

Into the deep, deeper water we sink and touch the edge of your chest with our tiptoes   When the days as long as tinnitus had passed we found ourselves in your river mouth   Rain fell in the night and in the morning where the storm subsided we saw the ocean send up white clouds   Your smile like the cleanly washed crumbs of sand received us

ON THE RIVERBANK 3

The current pushes you so, but
you stay where you are
Your blues swell and crest but
you linger

I am with you
Pushed and pulled but
you are with me

Towed by you I
give in to the flow
O, how you tremble

SINCE SICKENING

I thought you were somewhere far But psoriasis and fever bloom on my skin and made me realize you're near With you next to me I'll want for nothing else You came to me fast but I've nothing to do or become I want to hold your hand and go far from here but when I take a step you step back, and when I take a step back you step toward me, because you know very well that if our bodies merge my love will wane

SADNESS

Would I want from you a path you do not make
Would you want from me a path you do not make
If a path I take is not a path toward you
do you walk it with me within me
To hate me and love you or hate you
and love me, these branched and stunted paths
are your sadness   Because of me you wane

CHAINS

When I entered deep inside you I was still outside you You seemed to smile and you seemed to cry and that sound that was many sadnesses and joys weaved into one spiraled out from my head to my feet Sunk in that sound I forgot myself and you, and the chains of countless reincarnations sparkled Between the sparkling came the darkness where you and I became strangers

SUNSET

I rejoice in the full love you give me   When have I even dreamed of receiving such love   I couldn't eat or sleep but only thought of you   I was like the tree lit aflame by the light of a sunset   The sun had set but not my love that set the hill on fire   Every blade of grass blown by the wind was an agony   Tread on my agony as you come, when the night is here my love is merely a tree asleep

BIRD

I gently shake the sleeping leaves   They wish to return to sleep, as I did the day you first shook my heart   I want to follow them to sleep   In my sleep of leaves, I want to cover your exhausted wings   And when I open my eyes I'll see you flap your wings and fly away   Like the day you first shook my heart, the leaves will tremble so

FOOT

If I reach out my foot I can touch you   That's where you always are   I try at first and decide not to   It'll only startle you   But if I don't reach out my foot to touch you how sorry you would feel   Several times a day I am about to reach out my foot but then I always give up

WAITING

I don't worry about what I'd do if you leave
but today and every day I only wait for you
I've no arms or legs to make my way to you
no friends whose words to pass on to you
and you've forgotten me in your wandering
Even if I want to see you I cannot go to you
but you can come to me anytime you want
Stay for as long as you wish to stay
I've no arms or legs to hold on to you
nor do I have the strength or heart to do so
I don't worry about what I'd do if you leave
but today and every day I only wait for you
to come from the hills that spill like landslides

CRYING

Sometimes I want to cry But I've forgotten how My arm wants to cry My shoulder wants to cry The sadness that hasn't found a way out all day clunks inside me I try my best to push it out but then I give up If that sadness is you yourself then what else should I push out I think the day you finally leave me will be the first day I can cry

DESERT

The world is full of things I do not know   I kept getting sadder You say it's not all my fault but without me how could the world become sadder   On the main road I saw someone sob   His shoulders heaved like those of a plucked bird   He saw me and said, Son, let us go to the desert . . .   I ran from him   The more I ran the closer I came to the desert   The closer I came to the desert the more it resembled you   If it weren't for you how would I have seen the desert

TATTOO

I became as cruel as you, even knowing it would sadden you   And all I was left with was loneliness   Your blood smeared on my hands   I pushed away everything that came from you and to you, and all I was left with was loneliness   A vile tattoo I had inked on your heart

FUTURE

When you're with me I'm always anxious I fear your future will darken because of me But when we are apart, it is my own future that darkens And so I cannot hold on to you nor can I let you go I always dread your leaving When I suffer like this you say to me, "You have no arms or legs, so I shall do the holding" I know you must leave but I cannot send you away

MIRROR

All day I am filled to the brim with thoughts of you I cannot erase you Is there an end to this path We are sunk to our waists in death I and you are both in fear Is there an end to this path If not this path is there another Are you blocking my path from me Am I in the way of the path you must take All day I am filled to the brim with thoughts of you You gaze at me like a mirror

SONG 1

O the one I love, I came here and saw nothing Aside from death I did not wish to show you a death that shines like the eyes of a skittish beast Death was inside my body and beyond it O the one I love, the song you sang as you held my hand was death

SONG 2

I listen to all manner of songs and sing all manner of songs but still you fell into my heart, I can't pull you up from there, nor can I erase your eyes that flash fire inside me . . .

DESTINY

O Destiny!

As you exist, I go
Several men slip over
the ice surrounding me

O Destiny!

A hand spread open for no reason in the air,
flowering trees remain encased in the ice and
birds flock over the snowy fields in search of food

O Destiny!

I lower my forehead and
watch your shadow as it approaches
I wait for your shadow to leave like a distant memory

O Destiny! O Destiny!

RAIN 1

Go, go, I shouted at you
and you went, keening
but at night you come to my window in tears

You hit the magnolia by my window
and hit the paving stones
and hit the garden wall and

when I open the window you leap inside
and drench me whole

RAIN 2

When I wake feeling you're by my head you're outside When I open the window you're past the falling strands When I run through the strands you enter my room while I'm gone And as you sigh whitely, touching my scattered clothing and blanket with your slender fingers, do your ears perk up at the sound of my sodden footsteps returning

TEARS

The tears that flow from your eyes are so transparent they show the color of your skin They shine through your face, the inside of your body They turn your whole body into a transparent water vessel in a peaceful tree They flow in a place where every struggle, every clamor has ceased They come from a country where every struggle, every clamor has calmed They flow from a star thousands of light-years away They have come from a star thousands of light-years away and have just now touched your eyes . . . Like that glint of light that has just breathed its last, I melt inside your tears

PARTING 1

You were sad so I thought we were parting But then why would the birds sing and the flowers bloom Your sadness is the mirror of parting When I look inside you, you look inside me back I cannot tell if I am you or you are me In the mirror of parting we have changed places When you leave the one who parts will not be you but me And to me you will remain You were sad so I thought we were parting But then why would we have become one

PARTING 2

You are happy still   For suffering is still with you   But someday when he leaves you, you will be unbearably unhappy   For suffering will move on with him

PATH 1

You go ahead of me
and I stand behind you

The path of you and me
was lament

Covering our mouths when it was too loud
and covering our ears when it was still loud

Tears erased our path
Tears swallowed our path

The path we could not finish
was the lament that faded away

PATH 2

Each step forward I thought was the last These last steps formed a path This path born from ashes, from stepping forth from death, is laid at your beautiful feet

You tread my path and grow far from me

ELEGY 1

On the blue springs where March came
I sent you off and
we forgot our words

I said goodbye,
and even knowing I would never forget
said we must forget, forget together

On the blue springs where March came
your bones were scattered whitely
Like the dead trees on a lofty mountain we
collapse into white

ELEGY 2

As the sky over the pines is still blue today,
even with nowhere for our frozen sorrow to go
we cannot throw it out into that blue

The new winter barley pushes its sprouts above
the harvested laments of its mother and father
It is stepped on and stepped on but pokes out its head

RED ROCK

Red Rock, Red Rock
You left me
those words

Red Rock, Red Rock
lays its head on the riverbank
and sleeps the long spring

My suffering of a season
now flowed away
O Red Rock whose head lay toward you

REEK

Spring grass thickened on the dike
The riverbank reeked

With your shadow on the sands
that shift beneath the water
the long spring river flowed

Reek, the reek
Inside the water
O, there was massacre

Fish left only
with their eyes

Were their eyes to them
so precious, was my love
so precious to me

WHERE THE WIND WENT BY

Ten more li to go and my leg might uncramp   On the path where the wind went by, the sand lay warmly like burial mounds and the dusty blades of grass raised their sleepy eyes at me   One sleep and this heavy burden, these impressions shall all be a dream, but . . . Where the wind went by, as I cover with my sigh the blades that raised their sleepy eyes

A SONG THAT CANNOT BE HIDDEN 1

In the dark water and in the bright fire
sorrow recognized my face
Holding flowers I could give to no one
on my journey, stepping on my shadow
sorrow recognized me in the end
A face and secret that cannot be hidden
From the moment sorrow recognized me
my secret became light, a shining smile
But I do not know the face of sorrow
for that is sorrow's secret
Sorrow has erased its own face

A SONG THAT CANNOT BE HIDDEN 2

That I am still sorrowful is because my love could not fill your absence   When yellow dust fogs the spring sky and darken the path and the village, I pierce through the heavy years and go to where you once sat   Should my love fail to fill your absence, sorrow shall fill my love

What love is there that isn't sorrow   You who are too early or too late, before it is me or before it is you, our love is sorrow

A SONG THAT CANNOT BE HIDDEN 3

I leave you to begin my long road home to you
Looking back we'll be as dolmens, standing at road's end
and between, a silent desert, never trod
My life lies like a dash between two different deaths
Looking back we'll be as dolmens, blinded by ancient twilight
I leave you for I found your long road home to me

A SONG THAT CANNOT BE HIDDEN 4

From the day I left you, you had a home   A home only you may enter, your grave

I could not enter this home   A home only you may enter, a home brighter for my leaving

From the day I left you, you had a home   A home with a roof of bruised blue and four walls soft as wind

I leave you to build my home inside you   A grave with a roof of bruised blue and four walls soft as wind

LIPS

Even long after parting my lips would not forget yours Even long after I'm deaf and blind I'll recognize your lips They are parted for they still long Until the longing ends they will not shut When my longing swells your lips will open and when your longing swells my lips will open Our lips are like two flowering trees blooming and unblooming as one

EVERGREEN SONG

A close look at an evergreen branch reveals leaves that do not belong   The evergreen's leaves are round and flat but the branch's are pointed and sharp

You are far away now but in the evergreen tree we're together When coming forth from me and sinking into you there are no longer dark sighs or forced tears

Have you forgotten our evergreen song?

BY THE STREAM

How could my brush with you be unplanned
It could not be only my memories
those of our parting and the subsequent wandering in the dark
As you are not wet by my body
I am clean   How could such cleanliness
be not shame   I dig a deep groove of sorrow as I
flow in your heart but you
ignore me   You gave me a flowing body
yet you are the center that does not flow to me
Should my flow cease your center shall dim
How could resenting you be love
Now I shall seek those that absorb into every bit of me
and I shall darken   To make your center shine
I shall be dirtied for all time

LETTER 1

I wonder if when I first loved you I was like a deep, deep seam of mineral The more the days passed, the harder your love became, and before I knew it I was here up high on Silk Mountain The leaves have fallen and the dying of people is so very far from me now

I love you,
try as I might I cannot leave

LETTER 2

I knew you would leave that easily
I didn't know you would be that hard to leave

I thought only the flowering trees would suffer
but even the trees that do not flower were grievous

This morning the white hairs
of an old woman in the front of the bus
looked like the fraying strands of straw rope

and made me see your thick curly hair
as it will be years from now

You whom I love,
never be far from me
I write you this short letter on a windy, foreign street

LETTER 3

You asked if everyone here was all right
I said we had no choice but to be well
As in a legend flowers bloom and winds blow
and the sea ten li away mutters
We wandered for a long time   For we hated
all that resembled us . . . Reluctantly reunited
we became close   What we discarded
reached us in a time of great hunger and settled within
You asked if everyone here was all right
Don't worry we have no choice but to be well

LETTER 4

Whether greeting you or sending you off, I am as sorrowful as a fruit tree resplendent with new leaves   Should you come to me   please gaze upon my rustling canopy

When my love flowers, my life will wilt and become as ragged as a tree harvested of countless fruit   Should you leave me   please watch over the desiccated trees I resemble

Like a woman caught disrobing in the night   I am often startled in sleep   Remember my prayer that ends as darkly as the abrupt ceasing of a child's cries   as I remember you on your journey

LETTER 5

It's a sadness to me that we are so far apart   Sometimes I wonder if the path I wander now is the wrong one to have chosen   But everything being so far away is a pulse of comfort to my anxious heart now   I will try not to write you any more letters   Here in this snowless winter receiving the quick breath of this young tree beside me

THAT SUMMER'S END

That summer the crape myrtle survived   After the storm and the storm after that   it hung on and poured out a hail of red flowers

That summer I stood in the centers of storms   That summer my despair burst out into crimson but still I weathered the wind and rain

The crape myrtle heaves but burns bright, breathing fire   When its blossoms ruffled my narrow yard with blood, my despair came to an end

A Note from the Author

I thought about sadness for a long time. I couldn't understand how sadness could stretch its tendrils so, all the way to the ends of the Earth. I could accept how sadness follows happiness, but I couldn't understand how sadness could leave behind even more sadness. Sadness seemed like a high wall that not even the wisest, the most well-versed in the truths of the world, could surmount. Then one day I met a young teacher who said to me the following. The sadness of the wise is complete in itself; it has no opposite. And this holds true not only for sadness: happiness, too, has no opposite. Or had I ever seen the sky throw a lightning bolt and turn angry? Or heard of a corpse that was sad! I had nothing to say to that. The sadness, which seemed like an insurmountable wall, fell away like a painted backdrop. The backdrop and the wall behind it were both illusions, and even if, like the layers of an onion, they were both the peel and the core, surely neither could be anything more than an illusion. And if this illusion was complete in itself—then how could anything of this illusion be real?

A NOTE ABOUT THE AUTHOR

Born in Sangju, South Korea, in 1952, Lee Seong-bok is the author of eight poetry collections, as well as works of literary criticism and essays on photography. In 2023 Sublunary Editions published *Indeterminate Inflorescence*, a volume of 470 aphorisms collected by his students at Keimyung University in Daegu, where he has taught creative writing and French literature for more than four decades.

A NOTE ABOUT THE TRANSLATOR

Anton Hur is the translator of Lee Seong-bok's *Indeterminate Inflorescence.* His debut novel, *Toward Eternity,* was published by HarperVia in 2024. In 2022 he was double-longlisted and shortlisted for the International Booker Prize, and in 2023 his translation of Bora Chung's *Cursed Bunny* was a finalist for a National Book Award. He lives in Seoul, South Korea.

A NOTE ON THE TYPE

This book was set in Eloquence, created by type designer Paulo Goode in 2019. This typeface gracefully balances a contemporary aesthetic with classical roots and is a reinterpretation of early Renaissance type from such masters as Aldus Manutius, Nicholas Jenson, and Claude Garamont, otherwise known as Claude Garamond. Eloquence features a large x-height, sharp serifs, and significant amounts of negative space inside letters, aiding in readability.

Composed by North Market Street Graphics,
Lancaster, Pennsylvania

Designed by Soonyoung Kwon